A gift for:

Jeanne Barritt

from:
THE MONEY
FAMILY
AUG. 24, 2004

Jeanne,
Thank you
for being a
special friend
& an important
playing
spiritual part of
our Lives!

WE LOVE YOU
AND HOPE YOU
HAVE A GREAT
BIRTHDAY AND MANY
MORE TO COME!

GOD BLESS,
THE
MONKEY'S
(Terry, Evelyn, Aaron
Azure)

A Birthday Bouquet

Picked Just for You

Illustrated by Beth Yarbrough

Celebrate this day...

in your

very own way!

is for birthday

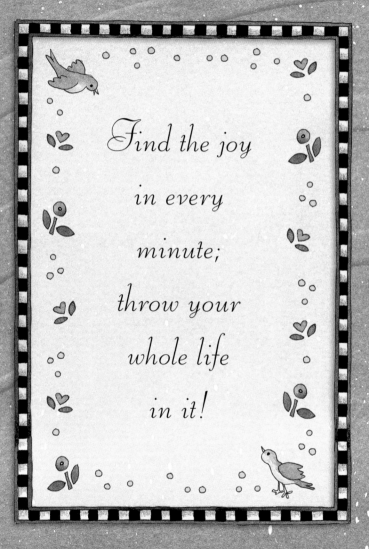

Find the joy

in every

minute;

throw your

whole life

in it!

HAPPY

A birthday is the perfect day

to remind you...

BIRTHDAY

how special you are
in every way!

Like flowers,
precious moments
can be gathered
from each day.

Life is so
precious a gift,
it is given to us
only a minute
at a time.

—Anonymous

A birthday is a good day
to have the time of your life!

Love, and do
what you like.

—St. Augustine

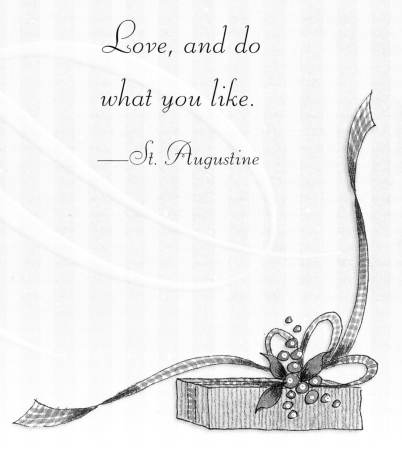

The most
valuable gift
is the gift of yourself.

—Anonymous

Treat yourself today:

- ♥ Eat some chocolate
- ♥ Take time to relax
- ♥ Enjoy a perfumed bubble bath
- ♥ Watch the sunrise or sunset
- ♥ Wave at complete strangers
- ♥ Drop all expectations
- ♥ Splurge on something for yourself
- ♥ Go fly a kite!

Make each
moment you live
the best it can be.

Make your birthday
a day to remember:

Do something silly,

Do something kind,

Do something fantastic,

Do something fun,

Do something hilarious,

Do something wonderful!

Life is like a garden—
the most beautiful
grows best
with both sunshine
and rain.

Birthday Wishes

©Beth Yarbrough

A birthday bouquet
for you today:

Buttercup
(cheerfulness)

Sweet Pea
(blessings)

Periwinkle
(happy memories)

Daffodil
(best regards)

Poppy
(extravagance)

Rose
(love)

Celebrate your birthday
with happiness and cheer.
It will fill your heart
with sunshine...

May your life
be filled
with laughter,
not just today...
but ever after.

God's blessing makes life rich;

nothing we do

can improve on God.

Proverbs 10:22, The Message

I pray
God's richest blessings
for you...
not just today
but always.

This day
is your very own.
May all the days ahead
be better than any
you have known.

Every
birthday
deserves
a party!

We turn
not older
with years,
but newer
every day.

—Emily Dickinson

Souls who

follow their hearts

thrive.

Proverbs 13:19,
The Message

May your birthday
be filled
with God's love
sent from above.

Happiness

is made

to be shared.

—*French Proverb*

God, you floodlight
my life;
I'm blazing with glory,
God's glory!

—Psalm 18:28, The Message

With every rising
of the sun,
think of your life
as just begun.

—Anonymous

Your birthday
is a gift to you—
one filled with hopes,
dreams, and
wonderful surprises.

How I
thank God...

for the
indescribable gift
of someone
like you.

May the year ahead
bloom with all sorts
of good things!

There are no
insignificant
people.

—Hugh Prather

What is the perfect thing
to give you
on your birthday?
Unexpected pleasures.

The heart of the giver
makes the gift
dear and precious.

—Martin Luther

No one
is born
beautiful.

It is
the gift
of a
generous
life.

Never let
your birthday
be ordinary.